1,000,000 Books

are available to read at

www.ForgottenBooks.com

Read online
Download PDF
Purchase in print

ISBN 978-1-5276-4668-1
PIBN 10172992

This book is a reproduction of an important historical work. Forgotten Books uses
state-of-the-art technology to digitally reconstruct the work, preserving the original format
whilst repairing imperfections present in the aged copy. In rare cases, an imperfection in
the original, such as a blemish or missing page, may be replicated in our edition. We do,
however, repair the vast majority of imperfections successfully; any imperfections that
remain are intentionally left to preserve the state of such historical works.

1 MONTH OF
FREE
READING

at

www.ForgottenBooks.com

By purchasing this book you are eligible for one month membership to ForgottenBooks.com, giving you unlimited access to our entire collection of over 1,000,000 titles via our web site and mobile apps.

To claim your free month visit:

www.forgottenbooks.com/free172992

English
Français
Deutsche
Italiano
Español
Português

www.forgottenbooks.com

Mythology Photography **Fiction**
Fishing Christianity **Art** Cooking
Essays Buddhism Freemasonry
Medicine **Biology** Music **Ancient
Egypt** Evolution Carpentry Physics
Dance Geology **Mathematics** Fitness
Shakespeare **Folklore** Yoga Marketing
Confidence Immortality Biographies
Poetry **Psychology** Witchcraft
Electronics Chemistry History **Law**
Accounting **Philosophy** Anthropology
Alchemy Drama Quantum Mechanics
Atheism Sexual Health **Ancient History**
Entrepreneurship Languages Sport
Paleontology Needlework Islam
Metaphysics Investment Archaeology
Parenting Statistics Criminology
Motivational

Stone.

No Compromise with Slavery.

AN ADDRESS

DELIVERED

IN THE

BROADWAY TABERNACLE, NEW YORK,

FEBRUARY 14, 1854,

BY

WILLIAM LLOYD GARRISON.

NEW YORK:
AMERICAN ANTI-SLAVERY SOCIETY,
142 NASSAU STREET.
1854.

No Compromise with Slavery.

AN ADDRESS

DELIVERED

IN THE

BROADWAY TABERNACLE, NEW YORK,

FEBRUARY 14, 1854,

BY

WILLIAM LLOYD GARRISON.

NEW YORK:
AMERICAN ANTI-SLAVERY SOCIETY,
142 NASSAU STREET,
1854.

1860. April 17.
Gift of
Henry Stone,
of the
Divinity School.
from
Boston

ADDRESS.

LADIES AND GENTLEMEN: An earnest espousal of
the Anti-Slavery cause for a quarter of a century,
under circumstances which have served in a special
manner to identify my name and labours with it,
will shield me from the charge of egotism, in assum-
ing to be its exponent—at least for myself—on this
occasion. All that I can compress within the limits
of a single lecture, by way of its elucidation, it shall
be my aim to accomplish. I will make a clean
breast of it. You shall know all that is in my heart
pertaining to Slavery, its supporters, and apologists.

Of necessity, as well as of choice, I am a "Garrisonian" Abolitionist—the most unpopular appellation that any man can have applied to him, in the
present state of public sentiment; yet, I am more
than confident, destined ultimately to be honourably
regarded by the wise and good. For though I have
never assumed to be a leader—have never sought
conspicuity of position, or notoriety of name—have
desired to follow, if others, better qualified, would
go before, and to be lost sight of in the throng of
Liberty's adherents, as a drop is merged in the
ocean; yet, as the appellation alluded to is applied,
not with any reference to myself invidiously, but
to excite prejudice against the noblest movement of
the age, in order that the most frightful system of

oppression ever devised by human ingenuity and wickedness may be left to grow and expand to the latest generation—I accept it as the synonym of absolute trust in God, and utter disregard of "that fear of man which bringeth a snare"—and so deem it alike honourable and praiseworthy.

Representing, then, that phase of Abolitionism which is the most contemned—to the suppression of which, the means and forces of the Church and the State are most actively directed—I am here to defend it against all its assailants as the highest expediency, the soundest philosophy, the noblest patriotism, the broadest philanthropy, and the best religion extant. To denounce it as fanatical, disorganizing, reckless of consequences, bitter and irreverent in spirit, infidel in heart, deaf alike to the suggestions of reason and the warnings of history, is to call good evil, and evil good; to put darkness for light, and light for darkness; to insist that Barabbas is better than Jesus; to cover with infamy the memories of patriarchs and prophets, apostles and martyrs; and to inaugurate Satan as the God of the universe. If, like the sun, it is not wholly spotless, still, like the sun, without it there is no light. If murky clouds obscure its brightness, still it shines in its strength. If, at any time, it seems to wane to its final setting, it is only to reveal itself in the splendour of a new ascension, unquenchable, glorious, sublime.

Let me define my positions, and at the same time challenge any one to show wherein they are untenable.

I.   I am a believer in that portion of the Declaration of American Independence in which it is set forth, as among self-evident truths, "that all men are created equal; that they are endowed by their Creator with certain inalienable rights; that among these are life, liberty, and the pursuit of happiness." Hence, I am an Abolitionist. Hence, I cannot but regard oppression in every form—and most of all, that which turns a man into a thing—with indignation and abhorrence. Not to cherish these feelings would be recreancy to principle. They who desire me to be dumb on the subject of Slavery, unless I will open my mouth in its defence, ask me to give the lie to my professions, to degrade my manhood, and to stain my soul. I will not be a liar, a poltroon, or a hypocrite, to accommodate any party, to gratify any sect, to escape any odium or peril, to save any interest, to preserve any institution, or to promote any object. Convince me that one man may rightfully make another man his slave, and I will no longer subscribe to the Declaration of Independence. Convince me that liberty is not the inalienable birthright of every human being, of whatever complexion or clime, and I will give that instrument to the consuming fire. I do not know how to espouse freedom and slavery together. I do not know how to worship God and Mammon at the same time. If other men choose to go upon all-fours, I choose to stand erect, as God designed every man to stand. If, practically falsifying its heaven-attested principles, this nation denounces me for refusing to imitate its example,

1*

then, adhering all the more tenaciously to those principles, I will not cease to rebuke it for its guilty inconsistency. Numerically, the contest may be an unequal one, for the time being; but the Author of liberty and the Source of justice, the adorable God, is more than multitudinous, and he will defend the right. My crime is, that I will not go with the multitude to do evil. My singularity is, that when I say that Freedom is of God, and Slavery is of the devil, I mean just what I say. My fanaticism is, that I insist on the American people abolishing Slavery, or ceasing to prate of the rights of man. My hardihood is, in measuring them by their own standard, and convicting them out of their own mouths.

"Woe to the rebellious children, saith the Lord, that take counsel, but not of me; and that cover with a covering, but not of my spirit, that they may add sin to sin.

That walk to go down into Egypt, and have not asked at my mouth; to strengthen themselves in the strength of Pharaoh, and to trust in the shadow of Egypt!

Therefore shall the strength of Pharaoh be your shame, and the trust in the shadow of Egypt your confusion.

Now go, write it before them in a table, and note it in a book, that it may be for the time to come for ever and ever:

That this is a rebellious people, lying children, children that will not hear the law of the Lord.

Which say to the seers, See not; and to the prophets, Prophesy not unto us right things; speak unto us smooth things; prophesy deceits; get you out of the way, turn aside out of the path, cause the Holy One of Israel to cease from before us.

Wherefore thus saith the Holy One of Israel: Because

ye despise this word, and trust in oppression and perverseness, and stay thereon :

Therefore this iniquity shall be to you as a breach ready to fall, swelling out in a high wall, whose breaking cometh suddenly, at an instant."

II. Notwithstanding the lessons taught us by Pilgrim Fathers and Revolutionary Sires, at Plymouth Rock, on Bunker Hill, at Lexington, Concord and Yorktown; notwithstanding our Fourth of July celebrations, and ostentatious displays of patriotism; in what Eurpean nation is personal liberty held in such contempt as in our own? Where are there such unbelievers in the natural equality and freedom of mankind? Our slaves outnumber the entire population of the country at the time of our revolutionary struggle. In vain do they clank their chains, and fill the air with their shrieks, and make their supplications for mercy. In vain are their sufferings portrayed, their wrongs rehearsed, their rights defended. As Nero fiddled while Rome was burning, so the slaveholding spirit of this nation rejoices, as one barrier of liberty after another is destroyed, and fresh victims are multiplied for the cotton-field and the auction-block. For one impeachment of the slave system, a thousand defences are made. For one rebuke of the man-stealer, a thousand denunciations of the Abolitionists are heard. For one press that bears a faithful testimony against Slavery, a score are ready to be prostituted to its service. For one pulpit that is not "recreant to its trust," there are ten that openly defend slaveholding as compatible with Christianity, and scores that are dumb.

For one church that excludes the human enslaver
from its communion table, multitudes extend to him
the right hand of religious fellowship. The wealth,
the enterprise, the literature, the politics, the religion of the land, are all combined to give extension.
and perpetuity to the Slave Power. Everywhere to
do homage to it, to avoid collision with it, to propi-
tiate its favour, is deemed essential—nay, *is* essential
to political preferment and ecclesiastical advance-
ment. Nothing is so unpopular as impartial liberty.
The two great parties which absorb nearly the whole
voting strength of the Republic are pledged to be
deaf, dumb and blind to whatever outrages the Slave
Power may attempt to perpetrate. Cotton is in their
ears—blinds are over their eyes—padlocks are upon
their lips. They are as clay in the hands of the
potter, and already moulded into vessels of dishonour, to be used for the vilest purposes. The
tremendous power of the Government is actively
wielded to " crush out" the little Anti-Slavery life
that remains in individual hearts, and to open new
and boundless domains for the expansion of the
Slave system. No man known or suspected to be
hostile to " the Compromise Measures, including the
Fugitive Slave Law," is allowed to hope for any
office under the present Administration. The ship
of State is labouring in the trough of the sea—her
engine powerless, her bulwarks swept away, her
masts gone, her lifeboats destroyed, her pumps
choked, and the leak gaining rapidly upon her; and
as wave after wave dashes over her, all that might

otherwise serve to keep her afloat is swallowed by the remorseless deep. God of heaven! if the ship is destined to go down " full many a fathom deep," is every soul on board to perish? Ho! a sail! a sail! The weather-beaten, but staunch ship Abolition, commanded by the Genius of Liberty, is bearing towards the wreck, with the cheering motto, inscribed in legible capitals, " WE WILL NOT FORSAKE YOU!" Let us hope, even against hope, that rescue is not wholly impossible.

To drop what is figurative for the actual. I have expressed the belief that, so lost to all self-respect and all ideas of justice have we become by the corrupting presence of Slavery, in no European nation is personal liberty held at such discount, as a matter of principle, as in our own. See how clearly this is demonstrated. The reasons adduced among us in justication of slaveholding, and therefore against personal liberty, are multitudinous. I will enumerate only a dozen of these: 1. " The victims are black." 2. " The slaves belong to an inferior race." 3. " Many of them have been fairly purchased." 4. "Others have been honestly inherited." 5. "Their emancipation would impoverish their owners." 6. "They are better off as slaves than they would be as freemen." 7. " They could not take care of themselves if set free." 8. " Their simultaneous liberation would be attended with great danger." 9. " Any interference in their behalf will excite the ill-will of the South, and thus seriously affect Northern trade and commerce." 10. " The Union can be preserved only by letting Slavery alone, and that is of paramount importance." 11. "Slavery is a lawful and constitutional system, and therefore not a crime." 12. "Slavery is sanctioned by the Bible; the Bible is the word of God; therefore God sanctions Slavery, and the Abolitionists are wise above what is written."

Here, then, are twelve reasons which are popularly urged in all parts of the country, as conclusive against the right of a man to himself. If they are valid, in any instance, what becomes of the Declaration of Independence? On what ground can the revolutionary war, can any struggle for liberty, be justified? Nay, cannot all the despotisms of the earth take shelter under them? If they are valid, then why is not the jesuitical doctrine, that the end sanctifies the means, and that it is right to do evil that good may come, morally sound? If they are valid, then how does it appear that God is no respecter of persons? or how can he say, "All souls are mine"? or what is to be done with Christ's injunction, "Call no man master"? or with what justice can the same duties and the same obligations (such as are embodied in the Decalogue and the gospel of Christ) be exacted of chattels as of men?

But they are not valid. They are the logic of Bedlam, the morality of the pirate ship, the diabolism of the pit. They insult the common sense and shock the moral nature of mankind. Take them to Europe, and see with what scorn they will be universally treated! Go, first, to England, and gravely propound them there; and the universal response will proudly be, in the thrilling lines of Cowper,

" Slaves cannot breathe in England; if their lungs
Inhale our air, that moment they are free!
They touch our country, and their shackles fall!"

Every Briton, indignant at the monstrous claim, will answer, in the emphatic words of Brougham : "Tell me not of rights; talk not of the property of the planter in his slaves! I deny the right—I acknowledge not the property! The principles, the feelings of our nature, rise in rebellion against it. Be the appeal made to the understanding or to the heart, the sentence is the same that rejects it." And Curran, in words of burning eloquence, shall reply : "I speak in the spirit of the British law, which makes liberty commensurate with, and inseparable from, the British soil—which proclaims, even to the stranger and the sojourner, that the ground on which he treads is holy, and consecrated by the genius of universal emancipation. No matter in what language his doom may have been pronounced; no matter what complexion an Indian or an African sun may have burnt upon him; no matter in what disastrous battle his liberty may have been cloven down; no matter with what solemnities he may have been offered upon the altar of Slavery; the first moment he touches the sacred soil of Britain, the altar and the god sink together in the dust—his spirit walks abroad in its own majesty—his body swells beyond the measure of his chains, and he stands redeemed, regenerated and disenthralled, by the irresistible genius of universal emancipation."

Again—take these slaveholding pleas to Scotlar and, from the graves of the dead and the homes the living, they shall be replied to in thunder-ton in the language of Burns: "A man's a man, for that."

> "Who would be a traitor knave?
> Who would fill a coward's grave?
> Who so base as be a slave?
> Let him turn and flee!"

Pass over to Ireland, and there repeat these cuses for Slavery, and eight million voices sh reply, in the words of Thomas Moore:

> "To think that man, thou just and loving God!
> Should stand before thee with a tyrant's rod,
> O'er creatures like himself, with souls from Thee,
> Yet dare to boast of perfect liberty!
> Away! away! I'd rather hold my neck
> By doubtful tenure from a Sultan's beck,
> In climes where liberty has scarce been nam'd,
> Nor any right but that of ruling claim'd,
> Than thus to live where boasted Freedom waves
> Her fustian flag in mockery over slaves!"

And the testimony of O'Connell, in behalf of all I: land, shall pass from mouth to mouth: "I am Abolitionist. I am for speedy, immediate Abolitic I care not what caste, creed or colour, Slavery m assume. Whether it be personal or political, men or corporeal, intellectual or spiritual, I am for instant, its total Abolition. I am for justice, in t name of humanity, and according to the law of t living God." "Let none of the slave-owners, deal in human flesh, dare to set a foot upon our free soil "We are all children of the same Creator, heirs the same promise, purchased by the blood of t same Redeemer—and what signifies of what cas colour or creed we may be? It is our duty to pi claim that the cause of the negro is our cause, and that we will insist upon doing away, to the best of our human ability, the stain of Slavery, not only from every portion of this mighty empire, but from the whole face of the earth." "Let the American Abolitionists be honoured in proportion as the slaveholders are execrated."

Pass over to the Continent, even into Papal-ridden Italy, and there urge the popular pleas in defence of slaveholding, and, from the Vatican, Pope Gregory XVI. shall reply: "We urgently invoke, in the name of God, all Christians, of whatever condition, that none henceforth dare to subject to Slavery, unjustly persecute, or despoil of their goods, Indians, Negroes, or other classes of men, or to be accessories to others, or furnish them aid or assistance in so doing; and on no account henceforth to exercise that inhuman traffic, by which Negroes are reduced to Slavery, as if they were not men, but automata or chattels, and are sold in defiance of all the laws of justice and humanity, and devoted to severe and intolerable labours."

Proceed to Austria, and there defend the practice of reducing men to Slavery, and the Austrian code shall proclaim: "Every man, by right of nature, sanctioned by reason, must be considered a free person. Every slave becomes free from the moment he touches the Austrian soil, or an Austrian ship."

Finally, enter the Tunisian dominions, and there urge the claim of property in man, and Musheer Ahmed Bashaw Bey shall reply: "We declare that all slaves that shall enter our kingdom, by land or by sea, shall be free; and further order, that every one born a slave in our dominions shall be considered as free from the very instant of his birth, and that he shall neither be sold nor bought."

Thus do I prove that, in regard to personal liberty —the right of every man to the ownership of his own body—even Italy, Austria and Tunis are in advance of this boasted Republic, and put it to open shame!

III. The Abolitionism which I advocate is as absolute as the law of God, and as unyielding as His throne. It admits of no compromise. Every slave is a stolen man; every slaveholder is a man-stealer. By no precedent, no example, no law, no compact, no purchase, no bequest, no inheritance, no combination of circumstances, is slaveholding right or justifiable. While a slave remains in his fetters, the land must have no rest. Whatever sanctions his doom must be pronounced accursed. The law that makes him a chattel is to be trampled under foot; the compact that is formed at his expense, and cemented with his blood, is null and void; the church that consents to his enslavement is horribly atheistical; the religion that receives to its communion the enslaver is the embodiment of all criminality. Such, at least, is the verdict of my own soul, on the supposition that I am to be the slave; that my wife is to be sold from me for the vilest purposes; that my children are to be torn from my arms, and disposed of to the highest bidder, like sheep in the market. And who am I but a man?

What right have I to be free, that another man cannot prove himself to possess by nature ? Who or what are my wife and children, that they should not be herded with four-footed beasts, as well as others thus sacredly related ? If I am white, and another is black, complexionally, what follows ?

> " Does, then, th' immortal principle within
> Change with the casual colour of the skin ?
> Does matter govern spirit ? or is mind
> Degraded by the form to which 'tis joined ? "

What if I am rich, and another is poor—strong, and he is weak—intelligent, and he is benighted—elevated, and he is depraved ? "Have we not one Father ? Hath not one God created us ? "

> " How rich, how poor, how abject, how august,
> How complicate, how wonderful is man !
> Distinguished link in being's endless chain,
> Midway from nothing to the Deity !
> A beam ethereal, sullied and absorpt ;
> Though sullied and dishonoured, still divine ! "

Such is man, in every clime—above all compacts, greater than all institutions, sacred against every outrage, priceless, immortal !

By this sure test, every institution, every party, every form of government, every kind of religion, is to be tried. God never made a human being either for destruction or degradation. It is plain, therefore, that whatever cannot flourish except at the sacrifice of that being, ought not to exist. Show me the party that can obtain supremacy only by trampling upon human individuality and personal sovereignty, and you will thereby pronounce sentence of death upon it. Show me the government which can be maintained only by destroying the rights of a portion of the people, and you will indicate the duty of openly revolting against it. Show me the religion which sanctions the ownership of one man by another, and you will demonstrate it to be purely infernal in its origin and spirit.

No man is to be injured in his person, mind, or estate. He cannot be, with benefit to any other man, or to any state of society. Whoever would sacrifice him for any purpose is both morally and politically insane. Every man is equivalent to every other man. Destroy the equivalent, and what is left? "So God created man in his own image—male and female created he them." This is a death-blow to all claims of superiority, to all charges of inferiority, to all usurpation, to all oppressive dominion.

But all these declarations are truisms. Most certainly; and they are all that is stigmatized as "Garrisonian Abolitionism." I have not, at any time, advanced an ultra sentiment, or made an extravagant ⬤ nd. I have avoided fanaticism on the one hand, and folly on the other. No man can show that I have taken one step beyond the line of justice, or forgotten the welfare of the master in my anxiety to free the slave. Why, citizens of the Empire State, did you proclaim liberty to all in bondage on your soil, in 1827, and forevermore? Certainly, not on the ground of expediency, but of principle. Why do you make slaveholding unlawful among yourselves? Why is it not as easy to buy, breed, inherit, and make slaves in this State, compatible with benevolence, justice, and right, as it is in Carolina or Georgia? Why do you compel the unmasked refugee from Van Dieman's Land to sigh for "a plantation well stocked with healthy negroes in Alabama," and not allow him the right to own and flog slaves in your presence? If slaveholding is not wrong under all circumstances, why have you decreed it to be so, within the limits of your State jurisdiction? Nay, why do you have a judiciary, a legislative assembly, a civil code, the ballot box, but to preserve your rights as one man? On what other ground, except that you are men, do you claim a right to personal freedom, to the ties of kindred, to the means of improvement, to constant development, to labour when and for whom you choose, to make your own contracts, to read and speak and print as you please, to remain at home or travel abroad, to exercise the elective franchise, to make your own rulers? What you demand for yourselves, in virtue of your manhood, I demand for the enslaved at the South, on the same ground. How is it that I am a madman, and you are perfectly rational? Wherein is my ultraism apparent? If the slaves are not men; if they do not possess human instincts, passions, faculties and powers; if they are below accountability, and devoid of reason; if for them there is no hope of immortality, no God, no heaven, no hell; if, in short, they are, what the Slave Code declares them to be, rightly "deemed, sold, taken, reputed and adjudged in law to be chattels personal in the hands of their owners and possessors, and their executors, administrators and assigns, to all intents, constructions,

2*

and purposes whatsoever;" then, undenia
mad, and can no longer discriminate betw
and a beast.   But, in that case, away wit
rible incongruity of giving them oral inst
teaching them the catechism, of recognisir
suitably qualified to be members of
churches, of extending to them the ordinar
tism, and admitting them to the commun
and enumerating many of them as belong
household of faith!   Let them be no mor(
in our religious sympathies or denominat
tistics than are the dogs in our streets, th
our pens, or the utensils in our dwellir
right to own, to buy, to sell, to inherit, to]
to control them, in the most absolute s(
constitutions and laws which forbid their
ought to be so far modified or repealed as 1
the right.

But, if they are men; if they are to run
career of immortality with ourselves; if
law of God is over them as over all other(
have souls to be saved or lost; if Jesus incl(
among those for whom he laid down h
Christ is within many of them "the hope (
then, when I claim for them all that we
ourselves, because we are created in the
God, I am guilty of no extravagance, but (
by every principle of honour, by all the
human nature, by obedience to Almight(
"remember them that are in bonds as b(
them," and to demand their immediate a
ditional emancipation.

I am " ultra " and " fanatical," forsooth ! In what
direction, or affecting what parties ? What have I
urged should be done to the slaveholders? Their
punishment as felons of the deepest dye ? No. I
have simply enunciated in their ear the divine command, " Loose the bands of wickedness, undo the
heavy burdens, break every yoke, and let the op-
pressed go free," accompanying it with the cheering
promises, " Then shall thy light rise in obscurity,
and thy darkness be as the noon-day. And the Lord
shall guide thee continually, and satisfy thy soul in
drought, and make fat thy bones; and thou shalt
be like a watered garden, and like a spring of water
whose waters fail not. And they that shall be of
thee shall build the old waste places; thou shalt
raise up the foundations of many generations ; and
thou shalt be called, The repairer of the breach, The
restorer of paths to dwell in." Yet, if I had affirmed
that they ought to meet the doom of pirates, I should
have been no more personal, no more merciless, than
is the law of Congress, making it a piratical act to
enslave a native African, under whatever pretence
or circumstances; for in the eye of reason, and by
the standard of eternal justice, it is as great a crime
to enslave one born on our own soil, as on the coast
of Africa; and as, in the latter case, neither the
plea of having fairly purchased or inherited him,
nor the pretence of seeking his temporal and eternal
good, by bringing him to a civilized and Christian
country, would be regarded as of any weight, so,
none of the excuses offered for slaveholding in this

country are worthy of the least consideration. The
act, in both cases, is essentially the same—equally
inhuman, immoral, piratical. Oppression is not a
matter of latitude or longitude; here excusable,
there to be execrated; here to elevate the oppressor
to the highest station, there to hang him by the neck
till he is dead; here compatible with Christianity,
there to be branded and punished as piracy. "He
that stealeth a man, and selleth him, or if he be
found in his hand, he shall surely be put to death."
So reads the Mosaic code, and by it every American
Slaveholder is convicted of a capital crime. By the
Declaration of Independence, he is pronounced a
man-stealer. As for myself, I have simply exposed
his guilt, besought him to repent, and to "go and
sin no more."

What extravagant claim have I made in behalf of
the slaves? Will it be replied, "Their immediate
liberation!" Then God, by his prophet, is guilty of
extravagance! Then Thomas Jefferson, who wrote
the Declaration of Independence, and all who signed
that instrument, and all who joined in the Revolutionary struggle, were deceivers in asserting it to be
a self-evident truth, that all men are endowed by
their Creator with an inalienable right to liberty!
The issue is not with me, but with them, and with
God. What! is it going too far to ask, for those who
have been outraged and plundered all their lives
long, nothing but houseless, penniless, naked freedom! No compensation whatever for their past un-
requited toil; no redress for their multitudinous

wrongs; no settlement for sundered ties, bleeding backs, countless lacerations, darkened intellects, ruined souls! The truth is, complete justice has never been asked for the enslaved.

How has the slave system grown to its present enormous dimensions? Through compromise. How is it to be exterminated? Only by an uncompromising spirit. This is to be carried out in all the relations of life—social, political, religious. Put not on the list of your friends, nor allow admission to your domestic circle, the man who on principle defends Slavery, but treat him as a moral leper. "If an American addresses you," said Daniel O'Connell to his countrymen, "find out at once if he be a slaveholder. He may have business with you, and the less you do with him the better; but the moment that is over, turn from him as if he had the cholera or the plague—for there is a moral cholera and a political plague upon him. He belongs not to your country or your clime—he is not within the pale of civilization or Christianity." On another occasion he said: "An American gentleman waited upon me this morning, and I asked him with some anxiety, 'What part of America do you come from?' 'I came from Boston.' Do me the honour to shake hands; you came from a State that has never been tarnished with Slavery—a State to which our ancestors fled from the tyranny of England—and the worst of all tyrannies, the attempt to interfere between man and his God—a tyranny that I have in principle helped to put down in this country, and wish to put down in every country upon the face of the globe. It is odious and insolent to interfere between a man and his God; to fetter with law the choice which the conscience makes of its mode of adoring the eternal and adorable God. I cannot talk of toleration, because it supposes that a boon has been given to a human being, in allowing him to have his conscience free. It was in that struggle, I said, that your fathers left England; and I rejoice to see an American from Boston; but I should be sorry to be contaminated by the touch of a man from those States where Slavery is continued. 'Oh,' said he, 'you are alluding to Slavery: though I am no advocate for it, yet, if you will allow me, I will discuss that question with you.' I replied, that if a man should propose to me a discussion on the propriety of picking pockets, I would turn him out of my study, for fear he should carry his theory into practice. 'And meaning you no sort of offence,' I added, 'which I cannot mean to a gentleman who does me the honour of paying me a civil visit, I would as soon discuss the one question with you as the other. The one is a paltry theft.

'He that steals my purse steals trash; 'tis something, nothing;
'Twas mine, 'tis his, and has been slave to thousands '—

but he who thinks he can vindicate the possession of one human being by another—the sale of soul and body—the separation of father and mother—the taking of the mother from the infant at her breast, and selling the one to one master, and the other to another—is a man whom I will not answer with words—nor with blows, for the time for the latter has not yet come.' "

If such a spirit of manly indignation and unbending integrity pervaded the Northern breast, how long could Slavery stand before it? But where is it to be found? Alas! the man whose hands are red with blood is honoured and caressed in proportion to the number of his victims; while "he who departs from evil makes himself a prey." This is true, universally, in our land. Why should not the Slave Power make colossal strides over the continent? "There is no North." A sordid, truckling, cowardly, compromising spirit, is everywhere seen. No insult or outrage, no deed of impiety or blood, on the part of the South, can startle us into resistance, or inspire us with self-respect. We see our free coloured citizens incarcerated in Southern prisons, or sold on the auction-block, for no other crime than that of being found on Southern soil; and we dare not call for redress. Our commerce with the South is bound with the shackles of the plantation—"Free-Trade and Sailors'-Rights" are every day violated in Southern ports; and we tamely submit to it as the slave does to the lash. Our natural, God-given right of free-speech, though constitutionally recognised as sacred in every part of the country, can be exercised in the slaveholding States only at the peril of our lives. Slavery cannot bear one ray of light, or the slightest criticism. "The character of Slavery," says Gov. Swain, of North Carolina, "is not to be discussed"—meaning at the

South. But he goes beyond this, and adds, "We
have an indubitable right to demand of the Free
States to suppress such discussion, totally and
promptly." Gov. Tazewell, of Virginia, makes the
same declaration. Gov. Lumpkin, of Georgia, says :
" The weapons of reason and argument are insuffi-
cient to put down discussion ; we can therefore hear
no argument upon the subject, for our opinions are
unalterably fixed." And he adds, that the Slave
States " will provide for their own protection, and
those who speak against Slavery will do well to
keep out of their bounds, or they will punish them."
The Charleston Courier declares, " The gallows and
the stake (*i. e.* burning alive and hanging) await
the Abolitionists who shall dare to appear in person
among us." The Columbia *Telescope* says : "Let us
declare through the public journals of our country,
that the question of Slavery is not and shall not be
open to discussion ; that the system is too deep-
rooted among us, and must remain forever ; that the
very moment any private individual attempts to lecture us upon its evils and immorality, and the necessity of putting means in operation to secure us
from them, in the same moment his tongue shall be
cut out and cast upon the dunghill." The Missouri
Argus says : " Abolition editors in slave States will
not dare to avow their opinions. It would be instant death to them." Finally, the New Orleans
True American says : " We can assure those, one and
all, who have embarked in the nefarious scheme of
abolishing Slavery at the South, that lashes will

hereafter be spared the backs of their emissaries. Let them send out their men to Louisiana; they will never return to tell their suffering, but they shall expiate the crime of interfering in our domestic institutions, by being burned at the stake." And Northern men cower at this, and consent to have their lips padlocked, and to be robbed of their constitutional right, aye, and their natural right, while travelling Southward; while the lordly slaveholder traverses the length and breadth of the Free States, with open mouth and impious tongue, cursing freedom and its advocates with impunity, and choosing Plymouth Rock, and the celebration of the landing of the Pilgrims upon it, as the place and the occasion specially fitting to eulogize Slavery and the Fugitive Slave Bill!

> "Now, by our fathers' ashes! where's the spirit
> Of the true-hearted and th' unshackled gone?
> Sons of old freemen! do we but inherit
> Their *names* alone?
> "Is the old Pilgrim spirit quenched within us,
> Stoops the proud manhood of our souls so low,
> That Passion's wile or Party's lure can win us
> To silence now?"

Whatever may be the guilt of the South, the North is still more responsible for the existence, growth and extension of Slavery. In her hand has been the destiny of the Republic from the beginning. She could have emancipated every slave, long ere this, had she been upright in heart and free in spirit. She has given respectability, security, and the means of sustenance and attack to her deadliest foe. She has educated the whole country, and particularly the Southern portion of it, secularly, theologically religiously; and the result is, three millions and a half of slaves, increasing at the appaling rate of one hundred thousand a year, three hundred a day, and one every five minutes—the utter corruption of public sentiment, and general skepticism as to the rights of man—the inauguration of Mammon in the place of the living God—the loss of all self-respect, all manhood, all sense of shame, all regard for justice—the Book styled holy, and claimed to be divinely inspired, everywhere expounded and enforced in extenuation or defence of slaveholding, and against the Anti-Slavery movement—colourphobia infecting the life-blood of the people—political profligacy unparalleled—the religious and the secular press generally hostile to Abolitionism as either infidel or anarchical in its spirit and purpose—the great mass of the churches with as little vitality as a grave-yard—the pulpits, with rare exceptions, filled with men as careful to consult the popular will as though there were no higher law—synods, presbyteries, general conferences, general assemblies, buttressing the slave power—the Government openly pro-slavery, and the National District the head-quarters of slave speculators—fifteen Slave States—and now, the repeal of the Missouri Compromise, and the consecration of five hundred thousand square miles of free territory forever to the service of the Slave Power!

And what does all this demonstrate? That the sin of this nation is not geographical—is not specially Southern—but deep-seated and universal. "The whole head is sick, and the whole heart faint." We are "full of wounds, and bruises, and putrifying sores." It proves, too, the folly of all plasters and palliatives. Some men are still talking of preventing the spread of the cancer, but leaving it just where it is. They admit that, constitutionally, it has now a right to ravage two-thirds of the body politic—but they protest against its extension. This is moral quackery. Even some, whose zeal in the Anti-Slavery cause is fervent, are so infatuated as to propose no other remedy for Slavery but its non-extension. Give it no more room, they say, and it may be safely left to its fate. Yes, but who shall "bell the cat?" Besides, with fifteen Slave States, and more than three millions of Slaves, how can we make any moral issue with the Slave Power against its further extension? Why should there not be twenty, thirty, fifty Slave States, as well as fifteen? Why should not the star-spangled banner wave over ten, as well as over three millions of Slaves? Why should not Nebraska be cultivated by Slave labour, as well as Florida or Texas? If men, under the American Constitution, may hold slaves at discretion and without dishonour in one-half of the country, why not in the whole of it? If it would be a damning sin for us to admit another Slave State into the Union, why is it not a damning sin to permit a Slave State to remain in the Union? Would it not be the acme of effrontery for a man, in amicable alliance with fifteen pickpockets, to profess scruples of conscience in regard to admitting another pilfering rogue to the fraternity? "Thou that sayest, A man should not steal, dost thou steal," or consent, in any instance, to stealing? "If the Lord be God, serve Him; but if Baal, then serve him." The South may well laugh to scorn the affected moral sensibility of the North against the extension of her slave system. It is nothing, in the present relations of the States, but sentimental hypocrisy. It has no stamina—no backbone. The argument for non-extension is an argument for the dissolution of the Union. With a glow of moral indignation, I protest against the promise and the pledge, by whomsoever made, that if the Slave Power will seek no more to lengthen its cords and strengthen its stakes, it may go unmolested and unchallenged, and survive as long as it can within its present limits. I would as soon turn pirate on the high seas as to give my consent to any such arrangement. I do not understand the moral code of those who, screaming in agony at the thought of Nebraska becoming a Slave Territory, virtually say to the South: "Only desist from your present designs, and we will leave you to flog, and lacerate, and plunder, and destroy the millions of hapless wretches already within your grasp. If you will no longer agitate the subject, we will not." There is no sense, no principle, no force in such an issue. Not a solitary slaveholder will I allow to enjoy repose on any other condition than instantly ceasing to be one. Not a single slave will I leave in his chains, on any conditions, or under any circumstances. I will not try to make as good a bargain for the Lord as the Devil will let me, and plead the necessity of a compromise, and regret that I cannot do any better, and be thankful that I can do so much. The Scriptural injunction is to be obeyed: "Resist the devil, and he will flee from you." My motto is, "No union with slaveholders, religiously or politically." Their motto is "Slavery forever! No alliance with Abolitionists, either in Church or State!" The issue is clear, explicit, determinate. The parties understand each other, and are drawn in battle array. They can never be reconciled—never walk together—never consent to a truce—never deal in honeyed phrases—never worship at the same altar—never acknowledge the same God. Between them there is an impassable gulf. In manners, in morals, in philosophy, in religion, in ideas of justice, in notions of law, in theories of government, in valuations or men, they are totally dissimilar.

I would to God that we might be, what we have never been—a united people; but God renders this possible only by "proclaiming liberty throughout all the land, unto all the inhabitants thereof." By what miracle can Freedom and Slavery be made amicably to strike hands? How can they administer the same Government, or legislate for the same interests? How can they receive the same baptism, be admitted to the same communion-table, believe in the same Gospel, and obtain the same heavenly inheritance? "I speak as unto wise men; judge ye." Certain propositions have long since been con-

3*

ceded to be plain, beyond contradiction. The apostolic inquiry has been regarded as equally admonitory and pertinent: "What concord hath Christ with Belial? or what fellowship hath light with darkness?" Fire and gunpowder, oil and water, cannot coalesce; but, assuredly, these are not more antagonistical than are the elements of Freedom and Slavery. The present American Union, therefore, is only one in form, not in reality. It is, and it always has been, the absolute supremacy of the Slave Power over the whole country—nothing more. What sectional heart-burnings or conflictive interests exist between the several Free States? None. They are homogeneous, animated by the same spirit, harmonious in their action as the movement of the spheres. It is only when we come to the dividing line between the Free States and the Slave States that shoals, breakers and whirlpools beset the ship of State, and threaten to engulf or strand it. Then the storm rages loud and long, and the ocean of popular feeling is lashed into fury.

While the present Union exists, I pronounce it hopeless to expect any repose, or that any barrier can be effectually raised against the extension of Slavery. With two thousand million dollars' worth of property in human flesh in its hands, to be watched and wielded as one vast interest for all the South—with forces never divided, and purposes never conflictive—with a spurious, negro-hating religion universally diffused, and everywhere ready to shield it from harm—with a selfish, sordid, divided North, long since bereft of its manhood, to cajole, bribe and intimidate—with its foot planted on two-thirds of our vast national domains, and there unquestioned, absolute and bloody in its sway—with the terrible strength and boundless resources of the whole country at its command—it cannot be otherwise than that the Slave Power will consummate its diabolical purposes to the uttermost The Northwest Territory, Nebraska, Mexico, Cuba, Hayti, the Sandwich Islands, and colonial possessions in the tropics—to seize and subjugate these to its accursed reign, and ultimately to re-establish the foreign Slave Trade as a lawful commerce, are among its settled designs. It is not a question of probabilities, but of time. And whom will a just God hold responsible for all these results? All who despise and persecute men on account of their complexion; all who endorse a slaveholding religion as genuine; all who give the right hand of Christian fellowship to men whose hands are stained with the blood of the slave; all who regard material prosperity as paramount to moral integrity, and the law of the land as above the law of God; all who are either hostile or indifferent to the Anti-Slavery movement; and all who advocate the necessity of making compromises with the Slave Power, in order that the Union may receive no detriment.

In itself, Slavery has no resources and no strength. Isolated and alone, it could not stand an hour; and, therefore, further aggression and conquest would be impossible.

Says the Editor of the Marysville (Tenn.) *Intelligencer*, in an article on the character and condition of the slave population :

" We of the South are emphatically surrounded by a dangerous class of beings—degraded, stupid savages—who, if they could but once entertain the idea that immediate and unconditional death would not be their portion, would re-enact the St. Domingo tragedy. But the consciousness, with all their stupidity, that a tenfold force, superior in discipline, if not in barbarity, would gather from the four corners of the United States and slaughter them, keeps them in subjection. *But, to the non-slaveholding States, particularly, we are indebted for a permanent safeguard against insurrection.* Without their assistance, the white population of the South would be too weak to quiet that insane desire for liberty which is ever ready to act itself out with every rational creature."

In the debate in Congress on the resolution to censure John Quincy Adams, for presenting a petition for the dissolution of the Union, Mr. Underwood, of Kentucky, said :

" They (the South) were the weaker portion, were in the minority. *The North could do what they pleased with them ;* they could adopt their own measures. All he asked was, that they would let the South know what those measures were. One thing he knew well ; that State, which he in part represented, had perhaps a deeper interest in this subject than any other, except Maryland and a small portion of Virginia. And why ? Because he knew that to dissolve the Union, and separate the different States composing the confederacy, making the Ohio River and the Mason and Dixon's line the boundary line, *he knew as soon as that was done, Slavery was done* in Kentucky, Maryland and a large portion of Virginia, and it would extend to all the States South of this line. *The dissolution of the Union was the dissolution of Slavery.* It has been the common practice for Southern men to get up on this floor, and say, ' Touch this subject, and we will dissolve this Union as a remedy.' *Their remedy was the destruction of the thing which they wished to save*, and any sensible man could see it. If the Union was dissolved into two parts, the slave would cross the line, and then turn round and curse the master from the other shore."

The declaration of Mr. Underwood as to the entire dependence of the slave masters on the citizens of the nominally Free States to guard their plantations, and secure them against desertion, is substantially confirmed by Thomas D. Arnold, of Tennessee, who, in a speech on the same subject, assures us that they are equally dependent on the North for *personal protection* against their slaves. In assigning his reasons for adhering to the Union, Mr. Arnold makes use of the following language :

"The Free States had a majority of 44 in that House. Under the new census, they would have 53. The cause of the slaveholding States was getting weaker and weaker, and what were they to do ? He would ask his Southern friends what the South had to rely on, if the Union were dissolved ? Suppose the dissolution could be peaceably effected (if that did not involve a contradiction in terms), what had the South to depend upon ? *All the crowned heads were against her. A million of slaves were ready to rise and strike for freedom at the first tap of the drum.* If they were cut loose from their friends at the North (friends that ought to be, and without them, the South had no friends), *whither were they to look for protection ?* How were they to sustain an assault from England or France, with the cancer at their vitals ? The more the South reflected, the more clearly she must see that she has a deep and vital interest in maintaining the Union."

These witnesses can neither be impeached nor ruled out of Court, and their testimony is true. While, therefore, the Union is preserved, I see no end

to the extension or perpetuity of Chattel Slavery—
no hope for peaceful deliverance of the millions who
are clanking their chains on our blood-red soil. Yet
I know that God reigns, and that the slave system
contains within itself the elements of destruction.
But how long it is to curse the earth, and desecrate
his image, he alone foresees. It is frightful to think
of the capacity of a nation like this to commit sin,
before the measure of its iniquities be filled, and the
exterminating judgments of God overtake it. For
what is left us but "a fearful looking for of judgment
and fiery indignation"? Or is God but a phan-
tom, and the Eternal Law but a figment of the ima-
gination? Has an everlasting divorce been effected
between cause and effect, and is it an absurd doctrine that, as a nation sows, so shall it also reap?
"Wherefore, hear the word of the Lord, ye scornful
men that rule this people: Because ye have said,
We have made a covenant with death, and with hell
are we at agreement; when the overflowing scourge
shall pass through, it shall not come unto us; for we
have made lies our refuge, and under falsehood have
we hid ourselves: Therefore, thus saith the Lord
God, Judgment will I lay to the line, and righteous-
ness to the plummet; and the hail shall sweep away
the refuge of lies, and the waters shall overflow the
hiding-place: And your covenant with death shall
be annulled, and your agreement with hell shall not
stand; when the overflowing scourge shall pass
through, then ye shall be trodden down by it."

These are solemn times. It is not a struggle for

national salvation ; for the nation, as such, seems doomed beyond recovery. The reason why the South rules, and the North falls prostrate in servile terror, is simply this : With the South, the preservation of Slavery is paramount to all other considerations—above party success, denominational unity, pecuniary interest, legal integrity, and constitutional obligation. With the North, the preservation of the Union is placed above all other things—above honour, justice, freedom, integrity of soul, the Decalogue and the Golden Rule—the Infinite God himself. All these she is ready to discard for the Union. Her devotion to it is the latest and the most terrible form of idolatry. She has given to the Slave Power a *carte blanche*, to be filled as it may dictate—and if, at any time, she grows restive under the yoke, and shrinks back aghast at the new atrocity contemplated, it is only necessary for that Power to crack the whip of Disunion over her head, as it has done again and again, and she will cower and obey like a plantation slave—for has she not sworn that she will sacrifice everything in heaven and on earth, rather than the Union ?

What then is to be done ? Friends of the slave, the question is not whether by our efforts we can abolish Slavery, speedily or remotely—for duty is ours, the result is with God ; but whether we will go with the multitude to do evil, sell our birthright for a mess of pottage, cease to cry aloud and spare not, and remain in Babylon when the command of God is, " Come out of her, my people, that ye be not partakers of her sins, and that ye receive not of her plagues." Let us stand in our lot, " and having done all, to stand." At least, a remnant shall be saved. Living or dying, defeated or victorious, be it ours to exclaim, " No compromise with Slavery ! Liberty for each, for all, forever ! Man above all institutions ! The supremacy of God over the whole earth !"

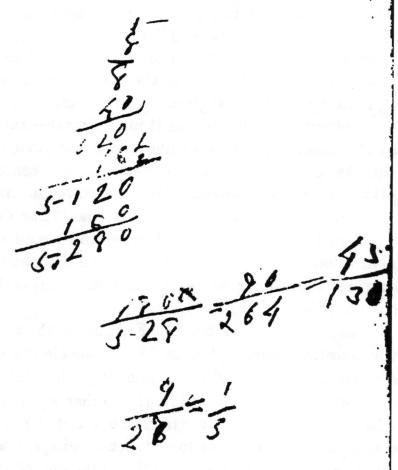